Shannon

Hope

Is the Thing with Feathers

Hope
Is the Thing with Feathers

BONNIE LOUISE KUCHLER

■ WILLOW CREEK PRESS®

Published by Willow Creek Press, Inc.
P.O. Box 147, Minocqua, Wisconsin 54548

Photo Credits:

p2 © creativ collection/age fotostock; p5 © Minden Pictures / Masterfile; p7 © Renee Stockdale/Kimball Stock;

p8 © Frank Krahmer/Masterfile; p11 © Ron Kimball/www.kimballstock.com; p12 © Sebastian Kennerknecht/Minden Pictures;

p15 © Klein-Hubert/www.kimballstock.com; p16 © Klein-Hubert/www.kimballstock.com;

p19 © John Hawkins/age fotostock; p20 © Ron Kimball/www.kimballstock.com;

p23 © Daniel J. Cox/www.kimballstock.com; p24 © Sergey Gorshkov /NPL/Minden Pictures;

p27 © Denver Bryan/www.kimballstock.com; p28 © Mitsuaki Iwago/Minden Pictures; p31 © ZSSD/Minden Pictures;

p32 © Patrick Frischknecht/age fotostock; p35 © G. Kopp/age fotostock;

p36 © Close Encounters of the Furry Kind/www.kimballstock.com; p39 © Jeff Mondragon/www.kimballstock.com;

p40 © Matthias Breiter/Minden Pictures; p43 © NaturePL/SuperStock; p44 © Alaska Stock/age fotostock;

p47 © ARCOC Steimer/age fotostock; p48 © Norbert Wu/Minden Pictures; p51 © George Sanker;

p52 © George Sanker; p55 © Tom & Pat Leeson/www.kimballstock.com; p56 © Juniors Bildarchiv/age fotostock;

p59 © Ryukichi Kameda/ Nature Production/Minden Pictures; p60 © Malcolm Schuyl/Minden Pictures;

p63 © Heidi & Hans-Juergen Koch/Minden Pictures; p64 © Ron Kimball/www.kimballstock.com;

p67 © Konrad Wothe/Minden Pictures; p68 © Cyril Ruoso/JH Editorial/Minden Pictures; p71 © Ch'ien Lee/Minden Pictures;

p72 © Lisa & Mike Husar/TeamHusar.com; p75 © Sumio Harada/Minden Pictures; p76 © Stephen Dalton/Minden Pictures;

p79 © David Tipling / age fotostock; p80 © Wild Wonders of Europe/ Zankl/NPL/Minden Pictures;

p83 © Pacific Stock/SuperStock; p84 © Tony Heald/npl/Minden Pictures; p87 © Flirt/SuperStock;

p88 © H. Schmidbauer/age fotostock; p91 © Daniel J. Cox/www.kimballstock.com;

p92 © Rob Reijnen/ Foto Natura/Minden Pictures; p95 © Dirscherl Reinhard/age fotostock;

p96 © Klein-Hubert/www.kimballstock.com;

Design: Donnie Rubo
Printed in China

for Betsy,

who could have given up hope,

but instead gave hope to those around her.

In memory of her remarkable, and only, son—

Capt. Joseph William Schultz.

We will never forget.

Hope

cannot be lost.

It can be muffled, sat on, snubbed,
or even pushed away,
but hope is always within reach.

Hope does not die, either.

Strangle it, smother it, and
thoroughly pummel it,
but hope is still there, waiting patiently
for a single flight of your imagination.

Life without

hope

is a biscuit without

baking powder.

—BONNIE LOUISE KUCHLER

It's not easy taking my problems

one at a time

when they refuse to get in line.

—ASHLEIGH BRILLIANT, AMERICAN CARTOONIST

Sometimes you need to hang
on to someone else's hope,
someone else's peace
❧ — and sanity, — ☙
while yours is under siege.

—LINDA MUNDY

*When you get to the
end of your rope,*

tie a knot

and hang on.

—FRANKLIN D. ROOSEVELT (1882-1945), 32ND US PRESIDENT

Most of the important things in the world
have been accomplished by people who

— **kept on trying** *—*

when there seemed to be no hope at all

—DALE CARNEGIE (1888-1955), AMERICAN AUTHOR AND SPEAKER

The mark of a great

fighter

is how he acts when

he is getting licked

—SUGAR RAY ROBINSON (1921-1989), AMERICAN BOXER

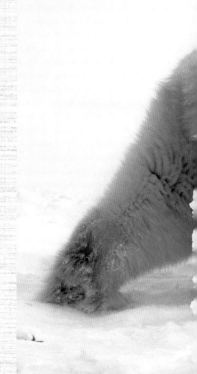

O Great Spirit, I seek
strength,
not to be greater than another,
but to fight my greatest
enemy—myself.

—FROM A NATIVE AMERICAN PRAYER

The most beautiful people we have known
are those who have known defeat,
known suffering, known struggle, known loss,
and have found their way out of the depths . . .
⊰ — Beautiful people — ⊱
do not just happen.

—DR. ELISABETH KÜBLER-ROSS, SWISS PSYCHIATRIST AND AUTHOR

Defeat may serve as well
as victory
to shake the soul and let the glory out.

—EDWIN MARKHAM (1852-1940), AMERICAN POET

Anyone who has never made a

⎯⎯ *mistake* ⎯⎯

has never tried anything new.

—ALBERT EINSTEIN (1879-1955), GERMAN-BORN
AMERICAN PHYSICIST, MATHEMATICIAN, INVENTOR

If you
fall,
fall forward

—UNKNOWN AUTHOR

If you fall seven times, ～ **stand up** ～ *eight.*

—JAPANESE PROVERB

Your heart
is greater than your wounds.

—HENRI J. M. NOUWEN (1932-1996), DUTCH AUTHOR, TEACHER, PRIEST

Happiness

often sneaks in through a door
you didn't know you left open.

—JOHN BARRYMORE (1882-1942), AMERICAN ACTOR

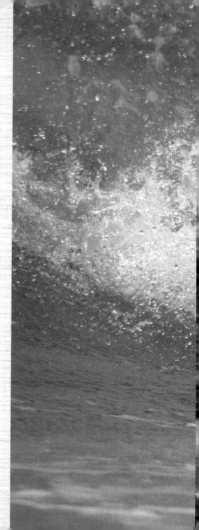

Hope is not a bridge over troubled water; it's a — **sturdy** — *little boat with oars.*

—BONNIE LOUISE KUCHLER

*If flowers can grow in
the crack of a rock,
then hope, too, can
grow
in a broken heart.*

—BONNIE LOUISE KUCHLER

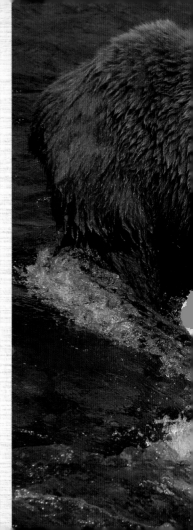

~ Hope ~

*affects everything; let your
hook always be cast.
In the stream where you
least expect it,
there will be a fish.*

—OVID (43 BC – AD C. 17), ROMAN POET

We cannot direct
the wind, but we can
❧— *adjust* —❧
the sails.

—UNKNOWN AUTHOR

If there is no wind,

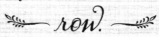 *row.*

—LATIN PROVERB

I am not afraid
of storms, for I am
learning how to

❧ — *sail* — ❧

my ship.

—LOUISA MAY ALCOTT (1832-1888),
AMERICAN NOVELIST

~ *Courage* ~

*is doing what you're
afraid to do. There can be no
courage unless you're scared*

—CAPTAIN EDWARD "EDDIE" VERNON RICKENBACKER (1890-1973), AMERICAN WWI FIGHTER ACE

Stop to look

fear

in the face.
You must do
the thing which
you think you
cannot do.

—ELEANOR ROOSEVELT (1884-1962), US FIRST LADY AND HUMANITARIAN

Sometimes even to

live

is an act of courage.

—SENECA THE YOUNGER (C. 3 BC – AD 65), ROMAN
PHILOSOPHER, DRAMATIST, STATESMAN

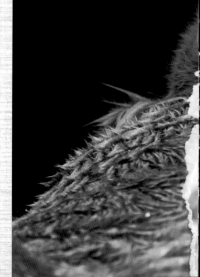

Fear will toss you, turn you,
and fling you out of bed;
~ *but hope* ~
is a feather pillow.

—BONNIE LOUISE KUCHLER

Hope begins in the dark,
the stubborn hope that if you
just show up and try to do the right thing,
the dawn will come.

—ANNE LAMOTT, AMERICAN AUTHOR

Hope is a

blossom

that pokes through the snow,
while spring lies silent
under a heavy blanket
and cannot be waked

—BONNIE LOUISE KUCHLER

Hope is the only bee that makes

~— *honey* —~

without flowers.

—ROBERT GREEN INGERSOLL (1833-1899), AMERICAN AUTHOR, TEACHER, STATESMAN

We will either find a way, or — *make one.* —

—HANNIBAL (247-183 BC), CARTHAGINIAN MILITARY LEADER

Hope

has little to do with logic.

—BONNIE LOUISE KUCHLER

Hope is the thing that pulls you to the

top of the hill

when you don't know what's

waiting on the other side.

—BONNIE LOUISE KUCHLER

The
journey
of a thousand miles
begins with one step.

—LAO TZU (145-86 BC), CHINESE PHILOSOPHER

Hope counts on
one sure thing:

change.

Hope knows you
will not be stuck
here, like this, forever.

—BONNIE LOUISE KUCHLER

— *Hope* —

is the feeling we have
that the feeling we have
is not permanent.

—MIGNON MCLAUGHLIN (1913-1983), AMERICAN JOURNALIST AND AUTHOR

Life

is a growth stage I'm going through.

—ATTRIBUTED TO ELLEN GOODMAN, AMERICAN COLUMNIST

*One can never consent to creep
when one feels the impulse
to soar.*

—HELEN KELLER (1880-1968), AMERICAN DEAF,
BLIND AUTHOR AND LECTURER

And the day came
when the risk to remain
tight inside the bud
was more painful
than the risk it took

to blossom.

—ANAÏS NIN (1903-1977), FRENCH AUTHOR AND DIARIST

Twenty years from now
you will be more disappointed by the things
that you didn't do than by the ones you did do.
So throw off the bowlines.
Sail away from the safe harbor.
Catch the trade winds in your sails.

Explore. Dream. Discover.

—MARK TWAIN (1835-1910), AMERICAN AUTHOR AND HUMORIST

Life can only be understood backwards;
but it must be lived

forwards.

—SØREN KIERKEGAARD (1813-1855), DANISH PHILOSOPHER, THEOLOGIAN, AUTHOR

Life loves

to be taken by the lapel and told
"I'm with you kid. Let's go."

—DR. MAYA ANGELOU, AMERICAN AUTOBIOGRAPHER AND POET

We're fools whether we dance
or not, so we might as well
dance.

—JAPANESE PROVERB

There is a need to find and sing our

~ *own song,* ~

to stretch our limbs and shake
them in a dance so wild that
nothing can roost there.

—BARBARA LAZEAR ASCHER

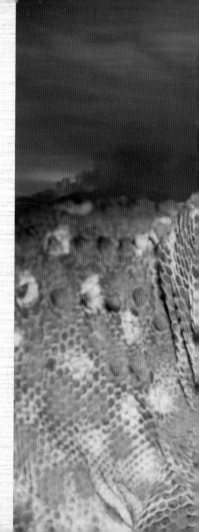

Life
is a great big canvas;
throw all the paint on it you can.

—DANNY KAYE (1913-1987), AMERICAN ACTOR

Hope is the thing with feathers
That perches in the soul,
And sings the tune without the words,
And never stops at all.

—EMILY DICKINSON (1830-1886), AMERICAN POET